I0756252

FINISHING LINE PRESS
www.finishinglinepress.com

# Relearning the Body

*poems by*

**Carlene M. Gadapee**

*Finishing Line Press*
Georgetown, Kentucky

# Relearning the Body

ISBN 979-8-89990-485-1 First Edition


ACKNOWLEDGMENTS

Some of the following poems appear in slightly different form:

“F Sharp” and “Flotsam” appear in *The Rumen*
“Mamie” appears in *Allium*
“Unapologetic” appears in *Verse-Virtual*
“Joanie’s Rant” appears in *Riff/t*
“A Page from Jane Eyre’s Diary” appears in *Poetica Review*
“BC” and “Talking to Keats” appears in *Touchstone*
“HOMECOMING TRILOGY” appear in *Backchannels*
“Relearning the Body” appears in *MicroLit Almanac*
“Free” appears in *Retrograde Review*
“Dawn Sky, December” appears in *Smoky Quartz*
“All Souls” appears in *MockingOwlRoost*

Publisher: Leah Huete de Maines
Editor: Christen Kincaid
Cover Art: Carlene M. Gadapee
Author Photo: Meghan K. Christ
Cover Design: Elizabeth Maines McCleavy

Order online: www.finishinglinepress.com
also available on amazon.com

Author inquiries and mail orders:
Finishing Line Press
PO Box 1626
Georgetown, Kentucky 40324
USA

# Contents

*"It's been a long time since I've been me." —Fernando Pessoa*

*"I dissent." —Ruth Bader Ginsburg*

*In memory of all women who have dared to write and to speak out, even when their efforts were not acknowledged.*

*In gratitude and love to my family and my poet friends. Thank you for trusting me, hearing me, and showing me how to use my voice.*

## Seven

Clock ticks. Cricket
chirps. Heartbeats slow
to the metronome
of memory. In sepia,
with dust motes,
golden:
a happy girl
in denim overalls
on a rusty
swing-set, braids flying.
She pumps
and pumps to touch
the sky.
Chains twist.
Red sneakers drag
in the dirt
again.

**Dinner,**

and I still sat, staring into the gray, watery stew,
broth grown cold and thin, carrots and mushy
green beans, pale onions flaccid in the murky,
shallow bowl, tough and inedible square lumps

of beef settling to the bottom, small land-masses
lifting out of the morass. I couldn't, just couldn't
bring four-year-old me to eat, to chew interminably,
to choke down flavorless chunks between sobs

and tears. Mother said I had to sit there until I
finished my dinner. And I still sat, after dishes
were done, the kitchen tidied, while night fell.
It was past time for a bath, almost time for bed.

And I still sat, squirming, my quivering chin
just barely clearing the table's edge. *Two more bites,*
my dad intervened. *Just two. Then you can*
*get down, get ready for bed. You can be all done.*

## F Sharp

Singing my alto part, *Cantate Domino*
learning the Latin,
weaving it in and around the desks,
the boots, the dust at my cruddy cleaning job
at 6 a.m., I belted it out *Canticum Novum*
over and over again, plunking that note
on my way back and forth
dragging the shitty vacuum cleaner. We pieced
our parts together, acapella—
soprano, alto, tenor, bass—
with direct eye contact and breath, *Cantate Domino*
tapping the tempo on our legs—

*Omnis*

(hold that harmony)

*Terra*

**After-the-Party Villanelle**

I'm mortified. I want to sink beneath the floor.
My dad is charming to everyone but mom and me.
My mom is acting like a drunken whore.
I never really noticed this before,
But everyone can hear him, and I'm sure they see
I'm mortified. I want to sink beneath the floor.
It's really not a problem, but my neck's a little sore
From going off the road (and I really have to pee);
My mom is acting like a drunken whore.
I feel sick. Why did I ever open up that door?
It's not anywhere I really want to be.
I'm mortified. I want to sink beneath the floor.
And then—that smirking frat boy followed me
And shoved his gross tongue down my throat, full bore!
(My mom is acting like a drunken whore.)
He called me beautiful, but I'm shaken to the core.
Why did I drink champagne? I want to flee:
I'm mortified. I want to sink beneath the floor.
My mom (and maybe *I* am?) acting like a drunken whore.

## Beer and St. Thomas

*"To one who has faith, no explanation is necessary."*

I got an email invitation to have "Pints with Aquinas,"
and I grimaced before I grinned. Catholic guilt wrestled
with irony, and the absurdity of the situation won.

Young Thomas chose the Dominicans; his noble family
had a much different life in mind. They deployed threats
and his brothers, but imprisoned, tempted, then caught
in a mystic rapture, he became a holy Doctor of the Church,

a man revered. Would he appreciate us knocking back a few
cold ones, parsing out his erudition, his *Summa Theologiae*
defined and refined, spread under soggy paper coasters, mixed
nuts and pretzels? We struggle, a few sad and thirsty seekers
staining pages with melted cheese goo and burger grease.

## Mamie

*after Rita Dove*

has her armor on, a composed mother
of a murdered boy, a martyred son.
Day-dress crisp and neat, nails polished
and done, her hair set just-so. Makeup

not smudged with grief or anger.
She does not raise her eyes above
the tragedy cooling on the steel table,
wrapped in windings of cotton and grief.

Her mother's-gaze directs us to the scene:
her boy, the tiles, the metal racks and sink.
A body waiting on the next table, another
woman's son, perhaps, or husband, father,

lover, mother, daughter, friend. Another life
too soon taken, or given, to the angry world.

## Unapologetic

smart remark
fat lip
backhanded split          sarcasm
dripped out
with blood. Truth bubbles forth.

*Children should be seen and not heard.*
Poor marks for self-
control
chatterbox, motormouth, always

something to say. I learned
no one wanted to listen.

It took years,
found my voice,
stripped apologies
from my speech.

## Joanie's Rant

*after Lisa Taddeo's "Forty-Two"*

There's a wedding up in goddamned Brooklyn,
and I have to look beautiful. How many miles
do I have to clock at the gym? I get Christmas cards
from towel boys. My abs are flat—well, flat enough
for 41. Okay, 42. With enough body crème, blush,
and soft lighting, I can pass for 30. Yeah. Sure. Pass 30,
and head straight on 'til 40. Too bad I can't outrun
that bioclock *TICK TICK TICKING* away the months,
the years. Those kids whispering at Victoria's Secret?
Little shits don't know how much they will depend
on wired and wide-banded. Gravity's a bitch.
The ol' girls are good enough, my thighs are taut,
and my shoulders—lotion. Lots of lotion. Forty bucks
an ounce. Damn. There's that 40 again:
forty days, forty nights, forty men. I wish one would last
for 40 minutes. Either they lose interest or millennials
have no attention span. They call me a Cougar—
If I gotta be a member of that club, I'll look awesome
doing it. I haven't had a burger n' fries or a sugar cookie
in years. Looking good enough to screw is a goddamned
full-time job. I want to roll over and wake up to a man
who smells like sleep and last night's romp more than one
morning at a time. I want to kick boxers out of my way
to the bathroom, I want to move a razor off the sink
and have to shuffle male clutter to make room in the cabinet
for my eyedrops. My generation thought we could have it all:
career, freedom, sex on demand, love, and at the end of the day,
we'd have someone to talk to. We weren't entirely wrong.
I've got stuff.
I've got art, nice clothes, more shoes than I can count. Tonight,
there's that wedding. Should I wear pants? Dark stockings?
Aw hell no.
Red micro-mini and stilettos for the win. And I might win.
Maybe the bartender will be male. And hot. And young.
My father told me that I could do anything.
Check that: I can *do* anyone.

## A Page from Jane Eyre's Diary

How like her, not to use a fresh piece
of paper, a white, blank, untouched
and unwrinkled sheet.

*Why do you ask me*
*for my reasons?*

Small words blend into tiny crevices.
Dry creases crackle and craze
the yellowed and torn piece
of scrap. Faded brown ink bleeds
into shredded edges: an acolyte's whisper,
not to disturb but to be heard, perhaps,
as someone passes by. This forgotten,
leftover corner, is part of something larger
than itself. Than herself.

## Flotsam

Broken dolls bob and sink
and bob again, hair streaming
with weeds and sand. Don't
rescue them. Salty crust
of spent swells stiffens torn nets
dredged up from the deep.
Hold back the tide, repel
roiling waves and rising
floods of oil slicks and bracken,
clotted with debris from various
wrecks, splintered spars cast up
and out of the murk. I wait.

## BC

One month before Covid, I was learning
how to teach little kids how to pack
a gun-shot wound. Lock-down meant
hiding under desks out of sight
of an active shooter. We learned
how to use a metal coffee cup
as a make-shift weapon. We learned
how to exit a school under hostile
takeover. No one ever thought we'd
have to hide from a virus, that an unseen
predator would close the schools
and force us to exit, books and computers
tucked under our arms. We were heroes,
working from dawn until midnight,
tracking kids suffering from isolation,
keeping them as safe as we could. Who
knew that, with all the twenty-second
counts, that people would so soon
be washing their hands of us as well?

## Go to Hell

Take the creaking elevator to purgatory,
where an endless flicker of gray light
emanates from a buzzing fluorescent bulb
that winks and chatters like a crusty old man
shuffle-standing far too close at the DMV.

An Easter-lily layer of church-lady perfume
wraps your mouth and nose and smells
like the automatic sprayer in an abandoned
public bathroom piled with wet paper towels
and crumpled Modess wrappers. A cracked

payphone receiver dangles before you, a sad
weight at the end of a line that no one will
answer. You have to figure this out by yourself.

## HOMECOMING TRILOGY

### I.

*And Still I Wait, Unsuitored*
*With a borrowed line from Homer*

The winds are rough, the waves run deep,
And my lover heads home to me,
Whistling on the wine-dark sea.

What is out there for him to see,
Roaming the ocean, far away?
He's whistling on the wine-dark sea.

Golden-sand islands, seductively
Beckon to sailors, held captively—
Can he whistle on the wine-dark sea?

Where stout ships, skimming mightily,
Wander on waves, so wild and free,
Will he whistle on the wine-dark sea?

Will my lover sail back to me?
I wait and sigh, so patiently,
Alone—wind whistles on the wine-dark sea.

**II.**

*"Do not let her know everything you know"*
*—Homer, The Odyssey*

Secrets burrow a raw hole under the heart,
an itchy pebble in a sweat-soaked sandal.
Like lead bird-shot, its weight nestles
between C3 or C4, deep in the curvature,
compressing the spine. What do you know
about pain? Long pauses infiltrate like cancer
cells deployed and scattered, guided missiles
that find tender spots that cannot heal. Keep

your Calypso, your Circe, your singing Sirens,
your unfaithful sacrifices made to the gods.
I'll keep my tightly woven silence.

## III.
## Faithful

A grey-eyed owl blinks in the filtered light of dawn,
and pink gauze dissolves into shreds of night sky.
Athena glides in. Sulphur-smoke and vapor-trails
of prophecy uncurl and twine into corners and under

chairs. She speaks of truth, of oaths broken and debts
to pay. Crafty Odysseus committed the brutal mistake,
and suitors' blood, purple and sticky, pools and draws
flies, staining sacred space. Home denied, he must

shoulder his oar. This next inland journey should be his
last. Splintered wood reminds his hands the wine-dark
sea will neither forget nor forgive: there is no rest.
Penelope weeps and weaves and waits again.

## Everything but the Squeal

If I were a chicken, you'd eye
these thighs, a prize to be won;
these rounded breasts would be
just the right size for guests.

If I were a pig, you'd ponder
this belly, pleased with the fat,
bacon rendered. These cheeks
declared prime, a delicacy,

one not wasted on an everyday
Monday night dinner. I've a hunch
that my haunches, grown round,
would be measured with glee,
your lips smacking at the hint
of a roast with veggies and mint.

Warm-blooded farm animals
are honored for their shape,
determined by simple joy
and delight. But not women:

our softly feminine curves
are a deception of foam
padding and wire prodding.
A sacrifice, indelibly inedible.

## All Original Parts: 1965

We built ourselves from the skin-side out:
arch supports, padded bras, shape-wear
that vacuum-sealed our former meals away
from view. Pear-shaped, apple-shaped, flat

as a board. None of it acceptable, none of it
to be left unique. Fix it, form it, fake it. Hide
it from view. I wonder how shocked and
disappointed young husbands were, fresh

from the sacrificial altar, when bras came off,
girdles got kicked to the corner, and wigs
settled their perfect curls onto naked foam
heads permanently tipped back, waiting.

## What the Pharisees Did Not Say

He likes women. He talks to them, like they might
have brains, or thoughts worth considering. They
are unclean, like the beasts they resemble, wide
hips and straggly hair, all wail and cry, as though
correction truly hurt. Misguided, irresponsible, fit
only to breed and cook, clean and wash and stay

out of the way. Each one is worth little without
the livestock and land that come with her; value
lies in sons, not daughters. They cannot be trusted.
His own mother, it is said, should have been set
aside, stoned publicly, shamed for her evident lust.

His followers don't quite know what to believe,
and the women remain on the edges of conversations,
listening, always listening to his voice. No matter:
that voice will not bother us much longer. Too bad
we could not pin anything more on him than bogus
healings, teaching in public, rousing his believers

to cast off their humility and embrace a compassionate
G-d. We can call him King of the Jews, a rebellious son
of a suspect family, a leader of merely common men.
If he likes women so much, let him cry to his mother.

## **Women's Work/Women's Woe**

Unstrung, sprung, flung to dust
with hairy flies and lies, false tries.
*How does your garden grow?*
We know no boundaries but our own
pretense, illusion, like a gossamer
filament floating amid motes and lint.
No hint, just cobweb-sash, fine patina
of ash and sand that lands in window
casings and doors left ajar as they are.
Never done. Unsung.

## Like Sylvia, Before the Gas

*after Sylvia Plath's "Wintering"*

Don't worry, I didn't kill myself
yet again.
Cellar steps. Windows covered
with burlap. Stale. Unmet need.
Razor blue shards of broken glass.
Pointed reminders.
                              Stop time,
take one second more, slide those cool
blue splinters into your skirt pocket
to prick fingers, draw blood, to feel
wholeness in the pieces.

Imperfectly remembered, concordance
glows like fragments of cathedral glass,
shattered shards shining and silent-still
under silt and sadness.          Sink
into yourself, dig a hollow basement.

You pause every morning
at the head of these stairs. You
wonder what would happen
if you leaned forward                    *let go let go let go let go*
and fell
into the space between.
Such a fall would only break an arm,
not your neck. Deep breaths
with each halting step, you proceed.

(Would it make any difference
if the man knew that his wife
buys triple-bladed razors?)

(It's too much effort and makes too much mess
to use them for anything except removing
unwanted hair. Anything else must remain.)

(What if he knew that the frozen scream
beneath your smile melts in stolen moments.)

You won't tell him, and he won't notice: détente.

## Talking Back to Keats

*"When I have fears..."*

When I forget to be afraid of an inherited muscular dystrophy
that will rob me of movement, of blinking, swallowing, and finally,
of speech, and the BRCA2 genes that may be lurking, of arthritis,
of loneliness, of being left broke and broken, it is a lovely stretch
of time, a settled quiet. An involuntary smile comes to my face.

In daylight hours, I am more rational. There's no reason to fear,
there's no evidence of problems. But come nightfall, come three a.m.,
I panic-palpate my squishy breasts. I practice swallowing, open my
eyes wide, and wider, slow my breathing and plan advance directives.

I don't want my eyes fixed on imminent death. I don't want my brain
to reel with final wishes. Does my family know the passwords?
Can they manage without me? Will I bankrupt them, fighting the dark?
A rooster crows that he's made it through another night. I have, too.

## Relearning the Body

The sweet kiss of blade on skin—no,
this is not a suicide poem—
releases the winter in tidy swaths,

untidy, unruly, itchy hair, left too long,
like this season. It's been a while since
conventional upkeep ruled grooming.

Winter is too cold, too dry, and my vision
too faded for shaving unless I must.
Today felt right. Under foamy suds, I feel

my way along knobby, knotted vein-paths,
behind creaky knees and over wrinkled,
puffy ankles, rediscovering the contours

of my aging, hibernated self, reacquainting
by touch long-healed scars and bruises.
These legs have carried me a long way,

and must for a while longer. Pale skin
emerges in clear, hair-free rows under
the hot-running tap, strangely smooth,
not elegant. This is ritual, this is spring.

## Free

My father departed one spring afternoon, leaving an untenanted
husk of a human home while my neighbor's trailer was gutted
by fire. Held my breath to ward off the smoke and phone call.

There's a "Free Shit" sign on my burned-out neighbor's lawn.
It's not clear if *free* is an adjective or a verb, but there's an arrow
pointing in the direction of the remains of the trailer, charred

and melted, the blackened steps leading into nowhere special.
The fire burned spectacularly, right across the street from me.
Flames leaped upward. Billows of oily, black smoke puffed

and smudged the sky at two o'clock. The street was shut down,
except for teen-agers on skateboards cluttering my driveway,
gawking in the pulsing glare of red lights probing my windows.

Does a soul burn like those wispy Pentecostal flames flickering
above each Apostle's head, wavering on the penciled page of my
catechism book? Or does it flare, then wink out? I always think
of it as a blue plume, like steam, free to leave on the last breath.

## At Dusk

My neighbors' windows slowly emerge
from darkness, tiny squares or rectangles
of light and shadow, lined with books
or brown curtains, lamps just out of sight.
There's movement, a passing body, blocking
light, defining human-shaped space.

Surrounding trees blur into cloud cover, and
streaking headlights crisscross my half-lit
window, a pinpoint of light, my small desk
and my own shadows within neatly framed
by my own rectangle, my scrim of curtains.
My own darkness needs a defining shape.

## Dawn Sky, December

The horizon is a smudgy pastel of grey, orange,
and deep indigo edges, like when you lift the tiny
paint brush, water dripping down the plastic shaft
over your child-hand, and you sweep it in wonder

and frustration over the plain white non-sky of paper,
a single sheet torn from a cheap sketch pad bought
at the market, told to make it last. I wish I could make
this early dawn sky last, keep it pale and indistinct,

ahead of the bright blues and whites, the predictable
streaks of clouds and chattering birds. I like the simple
starkness of roofline, of chimney, of light-pole framed
by watery paleness. I want mystery, not clarity. Street
lamps wink out, and day approaches. My troubled
thoughts rise with smoke from a neighboring chimney.

## Three Questions

*after Monty Python*

*What is my name?*
I am hidden behind my husband's name,
one that replaced the one from my father.
I have no brothers. My father had no brothers.
The name died with him.

*What is my quest?*
My quest is contentment, to work with words,
to lift someone up. I cook a good family meal.
I fail something every day.

*What is the air speed velocity of an unladen swallow?*
Who asks the swallow if she is truly unburdened?
Things that make my heart heavy don't bend
my wing but may break my spirit.
Air speed velocity is irrelevant.

## Laundry Day

I walk through each day like a woman
whose arms are wrapped around a pile
of dry laundry, clutching and holding on,
dropping socks and underwear, peering

over the top of the pile, denim jeans
rubbing the tip of her nose. I don't want
to drop anything, but I know I will, and
I can only hope to get from one room

to the next, losing only a few things
along the way. I can go back for them,
once the load I'm struggling with lands
on the bed, one tangled pile of clothes.

## All Souls

Purgatory is a waiting room, like
at the doctor's office. Magazines
are creased and old, the address
cut off or blacked out. Faint music
blends with a disembodied ringing
of a phone and conversations too low

to make out, a white noise. Flip
another page, look at recipes or
haircuts, hints on how to get grease
stains out of lace tablecloths, or
glossy ads for extra-large things:
vehicles, burgers, or adult diapers.

Look past faces of tired newcomers
through grey air, and focus on a beige
door covered with a poster about
seatbelts. Remember those souls
waiting for admission to heaven.
Too late, *Buckle up,* it says, to *save lives.*

**Blessings**
*Leviticus 19:14*

May the things that make you cry come from beauty
and not deep pain.
May any pain you feel emerge from temporary loss,
not defeat.
May any defeat you suffer be replaced by crowning glory.
May the glory you achieve be earned through labor
and not by pity.
May bouts of pity stem from empathy
and not jealous critics.
May any criticism be a lesson, not a bitter dish to swallow.
May the things you have to swallow be sweet
and not be bitter herbs.
May the bitter things you're given remind you
where you've come from.
May the place that you have come from be a firm foundation.
May your foundation always support you,
even when you stumble.
May the things that make you stumble turn out to be only stones.

Poet and teacher **Carlene M. Gadapee** lives in northern New Hampshire with her husband, several fruit trees, and a beehive. She holds two Masters' Degrees (MEd and MA-LS), both from Lyndon State College, now Vermont State University-Lyndon. She teaches both dual credit and AP English courses at a small public K-12 school.

Carlene M. Gadapee is the author of *What to Keep* (Finishing Line Press, 2025), which joined her poems and reviews found in many anthologies and journals which include *Allium, Smoky Quartz, Touchstone, MockingOwl Roost, Vox Populi,* and *MicroLit Almanac.* Carlene believes in solid words, good coffee, long talks, deep silences, New England sports teams, the blue of summer skies, and wool socks. Poetry gives all of these and more.

www.ingramcontent.com/pod-product-compliance
Lightning Source LLC
LaVergne TN
LVHW090540110826
845146LV00003B/1196

* 9 7 9 8 8 9 9 9 0 4 8 5 1 *